History c　　　　　　　...s I was told many
years ago,　　　.., not literally true, I now
understanc wnat my informant meant. The fact is
that new evidence comes to light, that changes our
perception of history. Accepted beliefs suddenly are
overturned by new discoveries. So I make no excuses,
but where I have been misled and have in turn misled
you, I have tried to make correction with the latest
information. Tomorrow it could all change again?

All references to the National Trust in this book refer to
the National Trust for Scotland

Page 36
Reference to the A9 should now be the A 882
Page 8 and 9
Telephone for the National Trust for Scotland , Cullodon
should read 0844 493 29

David C Roll

ARGYLL ✤ PUBLISHING

© Text, photos and illustrations David O'Neil 2008
© Map on pps 4/5 Collins Bartholomew Ltd 2008
Reproduced by Permission of HarperCollins Publishers
www.collinsbartholomew.com

First published in 2008 by
Argyll Publishing
Glendaruel
Argyll PA22 3AE
Scotland
www.argyllpublishing.com

**British Library Cataloguing-in-Publication Data.
A catalogue record for this book is available from
the British Library.**

ISBN 978 1 906134 18 1

Printing: Thomson Litho, Glasgow

Contents

© Collins Bartholomew 2008

Cape Wrath
Durness
Keoldale
Port of Ness
Sgiogarstaigh
Portnacon
Cranstackie
Kinlochbervie
Achriesgill
Eriboll
Loch Inchard
Rhiconich
Foinaven
915
Tolastadh Ùr
Tolsta Head
Laxford Bridge
 Arkle
787
Handa Island
Scourie
Ben Stack
721
Loch Stack
Achfary
Tiumpan Head
Pòrtnaguran
Siulaisiadar
Point of Stoer
Eddrachillis Bay
Kylestrome
Unapool
Ben Hee
873
Drumbeg
Clashnessie
Stoer
Clachtoll
Quinag
808
Glas Bheinn
776
Beinn Leoid
792
Loch More
Lochinver
Loch Assynt
Inchnadamph
Ben More Assynt
998
Rubha Coigeach
Inverkirkaig
Suilven
731
Canisp
846
Duchally
Reiff
Enard Bay
Cùl Mòr
Ledmore
Elphin
Badin
Summer Isles
Achiltibuie
Stac Pollaidh
613
Loch Lurgainn
Invercassl
Oykel Bridge
Culnacraig
Isle Martin
Meall Liath Choire
548
Glen Oykel
Croick
Greenstone Point
Ardmair
Ullapool (Ullapul)
Glen Einig
Rubha Reidh
Gruinard Bay
Beinn Ghobhlach
635
Leckmelm
Carron
Cove
Laide
Coast
Badcaul
Carn
Melvaig
Aultbea
An Teallach
1062
Inverlael
Beinn Dearg
1084
Beinn nan Eun
742
Poolewe
INVEREWE GARDENS
Loch na Sealga
Fionn Loch
CORRIESHALLOCH GORGE
EASTER ROSS
Gairloch
Gair Loch
Mullach Coire Mhic Fhearchair
1019
Sgurr Mòr
1110
Loch Glascarnoch
Ben
Port Henderson
Red Point
Talladale
Slioch
981
Aultguish Inn
WESTER
Garve
Strathpe
Contin
Fearnmore
Lower Diabaig
Beinn Alligin
985
BEINN EIGHE NATURE RESERVE
Liathach
1054
ROSS
Kinlochewe
Achnasheen
Loch Fannich
Grudie
Loch Luichart
Sgurr a'Mhuilinn
879
Milton
Strathconon
Inveralligan
Torridon
Shieldaig
Sgorr Ruadh
960
Scardroy
Orrin Reservoir
Loch Damh
Craig
Balnacra
Sgurr a'Chaorachain
1053
Sgurr a'Choire Ghlais
1083
Loch Monar
Farrar
Beinn Bhan
Bealach na Ba
Applecross
Lochcarron
Achintee
Attadale
Loch Mullardoch
Glen Cannich
Cannich
Toscaig
Aonach Buidhe
899
Crowlin Islands
Duirinish
Stromeferry
Carn Eighe
1183
Glen Affric
Kyle of Lochalsh (Caol Loch Aillse)
Balmacara
Dornie
EILEAN DONAN CASTLE
Kyleakin
Glen Affric
19
25
37
10
9
18
17
12
42
18
16
18
15
6
18
16
12

Preface

THIS BOOK covers an area of Scotland that is within easy reach of Inverness: Elgin to the East, Ullapool to the West, and the Pentland Firth to the North. It also includes some areas that would entail staying overnight in more inaccessible places within the region.

The roads in the North-West, whilst not bad, are in many cases tortuous and narrow, entailing care and therefore time to travel. Because of the distances involved there are often long stretches of lonely moorland to cross to reach some of the interesting locations. Many people come prepared to camp; others come by car and stay at the bed and breakfasts and hotels to be found in the area. I have therefore included routes that would not be suitable for day and half-day trips from Inverness. These tours can all be accomplished with a one or two night stay at the right location. But even if just taken from the comfort of an armchair while reading this book, I hope they will give some insight into the beautiful and interesting places to be found off the beaten track in the Highlands of Scotland.

Inverness

THE CITY of Inverness, the capital of the Highlands, lies on the shore before the narrows between the Beauly Firth and the Moray Firth. The fresh waters of the River Ness run into the salt waters of the firth at Kessock beside the bridge that carries the road across to the Black Isle. Over the years, Inverness has grown into a sprawling community eating into the green hills on three sides of the original settlement. The old town still retains some earlier features, though most of these date from the nineteenth century.

The city boasts an Episcopalian Cathedral, south of the river, facing the Castle. The Castle stands on the hill dominating the City, occupying a spot that has been fortified, on and off, since the fifth century. The present Castle replaced the one destroyed by the Jacobite army under Bonnie Prince Charlie. It dates from the mid-nineteenth century and is currently used as administration offices for Highland Council. Below the Castle is the tourist office and Inverness Museum and Art Gallery. The city centre is visitor friendly, including a large pedestrian area and a shopping mall. There are now three retail areas around the city. The one on the Aberdeen road has a cinema complex. Inverness offers boat trips on the firth following dolphins, trips round and on Loch Ness, 'Guide Friday' bus tours around Inverness and out to the Culloden battlefield.

The south side of Inverness is bounded by the Caledonian Canal. The road from Fort William (A82) crosses the Canal at Tomnahurich, the cemetery that lies to the left of the road and covers the hill of the same name. On the other side of the road is Bught Park. The park has an athletics track and indoor facilities, and there is also an ice rink and swimming pool. Beside these sporting areas the glasshouses of the Floral Hall contain a variety of flowers and exotic plants.

Inverness boasts a thriving live music and arts scene and hosts large scale outdoor concerts which attract big names.

The central position of the City makes it an important touring centre for the Highlands.

Tourist Office: Tel 0845 225 5121
National Trust for Scotland, Culloden: Tel 01463 790607
Floral Hall: Tel 01463 713553
Dolphin and Seal Centre: Tel 01463 731866

Culloden

LEAVING Inverness centre following the signs for Perth and the A9, the road south is signposted to Culloden and Cawdor Castle. Follow the signs for Culloden battlefield and drive out from the city into farm country, with the Moray Firth on the left and field and woodland on the right.

The battlefield can be identified by the flags defining the location of the various units involved. The Visitor Centre is located beside a substantial car park and houses an exhibition and bookshop with toilets and restaurant. The eve of the battle coincided with the birthday of General Cumberland. It is said that the Prince having assumed command of the Jacobite Army, spent most of the night prior to the battle marching his men around the area searching for the location of General Cumberland's birthday party, without success. It was a tired bedraggled army that faced Cumberland that fateful morning.

It is possible to walk around the battlefield and plaques show the location of the various clansmen and regiments involved. The Centre runs guided tours.

National Trust for Scotland: Tel 01463 790607

Clava Cairns

BEYOND the battlefield there is a crossroads. By taking the right hand road it is possible to cross the valley behind Culloden, over a small bridge to the sign on the right for Clava Cairns. This remarkable site has a series of grave mounds and standing stones. They are said to date from the Stone Age. As the picture shows, the location of the stones is in a wooded glade, quite beautiful in the sunlight and the atmosphere is peaceful and calm.

On the way to Clava Cairns, the great red Culloden railway viaduct can be seen away to the left. The viaduct is one of the important Victorian railway constructions still in use in Britain. It stretches in a great line of red brick arches across the valley.

Culloden viaduct

Cawdor Castle

FOLLOWING the road eastwards from the crossroads, Cawdor is only a short distance from Culloden and Clava Cairns.

Wrongly associated with Macbeth, it's on the site of the home of the Thanes and Earls of Cawdor since the thirteenth century. This is a beautiful example of a 'lived in' Scottish stately home. A castle which has evolved, it has additions through the centuries, from its fourteenth century square tower to its surrounding sixteenth century wings modified in the seventeenth and added to in the nineteenth century. The feeling of a lived-in building is one of its most appealing characteristics. The gardens set off the buildings and are well worth the time spent walking round. There is a charge for entry into the Castle and visitors are advised to check with the Tourist Office before booking.

Cawdor Castle: Tel 01667 404401

Fort George

APPROACHED from the A96, the road to Fort George passes the impressive walls of Castle Stuart, seventeenth century home of the Earl of Moray. Restored in the 1950s by Mr Colin MacKenzie, it has since become a luxury hotel.

The road passes Inverness Airport before curving out through the village of Ardersier to Fort George on the extreme end of the point on the Moray Firth. Much of the original building and recreation facilities outside the fort have been dismantled signalling its reduced function as a military base.

Strategically situated beside the village of Ardersier, the fort was built in the 1700s as part of the chain of forts ranging from Fort William in the west through Fort Augustus to Fort George in the north. These forts were built to control the influence of the Highland clans. Of the three forts, Fort George is the only survivor and is in fact still a military base used for training. The Fort is also unique as the only military establishment that is open to the public. The museum is open daily during the summer and visitors can borrow an audio guide to direct them round the various sites within the walls. The Naafi is open and a café and toilets are available to the public. Facilities for disabled visitors include self-propelled chairs and a road train tours the area to a timetable.

In 1773 Dr. Johnson and his biographer Boswell visited the fort as part of their famous journey round Scotland.

Fort George: Tel 01667 462777
Inverness Airport: Tel 01667 464000
Castle Stuart: Tel 01463 790745

Nairn

A FAVOURED resort during the nineteenth century, Nairn has sandy beaches, a golf course and a sunny climate. Situated at the mouth of the River Nairn on the shores of the Moray Firth, its origins go back to ancient times. The yacht harbour lies beside the mouth of the River Nairn alongside the sweep of the beach.

The main town harbour was built by Thomas Telford

and the town is surrounded by woodland and pasture.

Once known as the place where the Highlands and Lowlands divided, it is said Gaelic was spoken in the South-West and English in the North-East of the town. Three miles west of Nairn is Auldearn. The dovecote can be seen, where Montrose raised the Royal Standard before the battle in which he defeated the Covenanters in 1645. The area has several sites of Bronze Age and other historic interest well worth exploring.

One of the most beautiful castles of the region is Brodie. Burnt down in 1645 it was rebuilt and restored in the nineteenth century. The castle is now home to a fine art collection of Dutch, Flemish and English paintings.

The National Trust operates Brodie Castle. Described as more of a country house than a castle, Brodie is typical of many of the castles to be found in this area.

Tourist Office, Nairn: Tel 0845 2255121
Brodie Castle: Tel 01309 641371

Forres

A PLEASANT town perhaps most distinguished for Sueno's Stone that stands on the outskirts. Over 20ft. (6m) tall, with carved scenes on one side and a cross on the other, it stands in its case on the eastern approach to the town. Dating from the ninth century it is believed to depict the defeat of the Picts by a Scottish army.

The town does have other attractions. The gardens along the south side of the main street through the town make a colourful contrast to the rather severe buildings of the town. For the golfer, fine high standard courses, and for those interested in history the ancient origins of the town provide a variety of sites in the vicinity. The River Findhorn runs past the town widening towards its meeting with the Moray Firth at Findhorn Bay.

The Witches Stone marks the site where witches were burned near the old police station. A plaque marks the place of one such burning. The Nelson Monument stands on top of Cluny Hill just on the east side of town. On the shore on the Western side of Findhorn Bay, the Culbin Sandhills are part of the shifting shoreline that in 1694 was the scene of a disastrous sandstorm that inundated the fertile landscape including the mansion at Culbin, former home of the Kinnaird family. Now reaforested with Corsican and Scots Pine, the sands rise to over 100 feet in places. Relics of the past still get exposed by the restless winds of the Moray Firth.

Tourist Office, Forres: Tel: 01309 672938
Findhorn Nature Reserve: Tel: 01343 557048

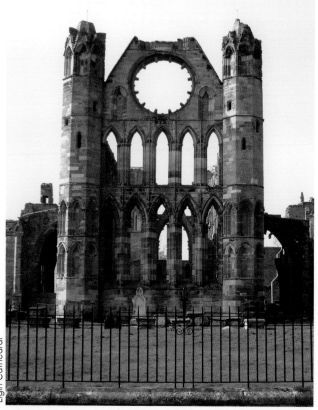

Elgin Cathedral

Elgin

ELGIN is perhaps the most famous of the Moray towns. Its distinctive ruined cathedral, known as the Lantern of the North, is regarded as one of the finest ecclesiastic monuments in Scotland. Encircled on three sides by the River Lossie, Elgin has a long and chequered history. After a serious fire in 1270, the redesigned cathedral was burned once more by Alexander Stewart, Earl of Buchan, known as the Wolf of Badenoch.

Though some attempts at restoration took place, by 1500 the place was allowed to fall into disuse and was once even used as a quarry. It is still a fine example of thirteenth and fourteenth century work as many of the original features remain.

Elsewhere in the town are other historic features: Greyfriars Chapel, the Muckle Cross, Thunderton House (now a hotel), and the House of Duff of Braco dating from 1694. Visited by Bonnie Prince Charlie prior to the Battle of Culloden, and Boswell and Dr Johnson in 1773, this town with its curious narrow streets stands now a mixture of old and new architecture on the road to Aberdeen, as it has done for at least 1,000 years. The Glen Moray Distillery on the bank of the River Lossie has produced quality whisky since 1897. Tours can be arranged.

Tourist Office, Elgin: Tel 01343 542666
Glen Moray Distillery: Tel 01343 550900

To Ullapool & the West

Ben Wyvis

FROM Inverness, the road to Ullapool can be either along the south side of the Beauly Firth or via the Kessock Bridge and over to the Black Isle.

Following the shore of the Beauly Firth past the end of the Caledonian Canal, as you reach the last lock complex on the right, notice the plaque on the cottage wall on the left opposite. This remembers Thomas Telford, the engineer responsible for the canal's construction.

Over the railway bridge at Clachnaharry, the road follows the waterside to the end of the Firth.

The countryside is green and fertile and the view along the water's edge, especially at low tide, is a busy scene of sea birds and waders investigating the muddy shallows. Leaving the waterside, the road passes the turnoff to Moniak Castle, the home of the famous Country Winery.

Moniak Castle

ONCE held by the Frasers of Lovat, the Castle was the scene of the capture of Simon Fraser. After the Battle of Culloden, he was arrested for his part in the Jacobite uprising. He was an unpleasant man who married for money, then apparently locked his wife in a dungeon under the Castle condemning her to a cruel death from starvation. Her ghost is said to haunt the Castle to this day. His end on the block was marked by an incident. As he climbed the platform, an old crone sitting by the steps remarked that he would soon lose that handsome head. His reply was that if he were as ugly as she, t'would be a happy day.

The castle is now owned by another branch of the Fraser clan. They have restored it and installed the winery, sauce and jam making equipment, producing the products for which the Castle is now famous.

Moniak Castle: Tel 01463831283

The Road West

THE turnoff to Kiltarlity is a shortcut to Drumnadrochit and Glen Affric. The main road passes through Beauly and the ruined twelfth century priory can be seen on the right. The priory was the burial place of the MacKenzies of Kintail as well as the Fraser and Chisholm families up until the 1600s.

Beyond Beauly, the road passes through Muir of Ord. Built as one, the village is of red sandstone. Across the railway bridge turning immediately left, the road goes past the Muir of Ord distillery and through the fields to Marybank.

Red Kites can often be seen hunting in this area.

The signposted right turn at Marybank takes us across the River Conan to the the main A832 to Ullapool. It has been known to flood at Marybank so it is worth checking before crossing. At the main road, turn left towards Ullapool through the village of Contin and pass the turnoff to Strathpeffer on the right. The War Memorial at the beginning of the village is a little different and is worth a second look. On leaving the village, the old disused bridge on the right, makes a nice photograph.

A few miles on, through Strath Conan, the country starts to alter from farmland to rather coarser woodland until it reaches the village of Garve. Here the railway literally crosses the road and the Garve Hotel can be seen on the right. In the car park of the hotel is a model of the lifting rig used in the raising of the Mary Rose. An earlier owner of the hotel was one of the engineers responsible.

From here the road divides – to the left the A832 goes to Achnasheen and Kyle of Lochalsh, Gairloch, Poolewe and Inverewe; straight on the A835 goes direct to Ullapool via Rogie Falls, Aultguish and Corrieshalloch Gorge.

Glen Ord Distillery: Tel 01463 872000
Garve Hotel: Tel 01997414205

Ruined Cottage

Achnasheen & Loch Maree

TAKING the A832 road, the first sixteen miles to Achnasheen should be mainly double width with possibly some remaining sections of single track still not upgraded, but not a bad road nonetheless.

The road follows Strath Bran past Loch Luichart. on the left, paralleling the railway. The power station on the right is one of the many hydro-electric units to be found in the Highlands. Of interest, the water supply to the power station does not come from the loch beside the road, but from Loch Tannich three miles to the north-west via a tunnel.

Ahead on the right can be seen a sign indicating a memorial to Captain Bertram Dickson (1873–1913), a pioneer of flight in Scotland. He was probably responsible for establishing the Royal Flying Corps and was the first pilot to fly an aircraft on a military mission.

Continuing on, the sheer loneliness of the landscape is impressive, more so knowing that up until the early nineteenth century, hundreds of crofting families once lived, loved and died in this country, only to be forcibly evicted to make way for sheep. At Achnasheen, the road divides once more. Ledgowan Lodge is at the crossroads to provide for refreshment and accommodation, if required, before the onward journey westward.

The road south-west is the A890 to Kyle, while to the west the A832 continues; some single track road should now be expected. Passing Loch Chroisg on the left, the road winds slightly uphill through green pasture and bracken. Then, round a long right hand bend, the road drops downhill through Glen Docherty to Loch Maree. Here there is a viewpoint and car park on the right. The view down the glen is breathtaking.

On reaching Loch Maree, the road traverses a narrowing section of pasture which becomes surrounded by the forest that dominates the southern shore of the Loch. The other (northern) shore is Slioch, over 3000ft of mountain rising steeply from the lochside, dominating the entire visible landscape. A favourite with climbers and walkers alike, the combination of mountain, loch, moor and forest makes this area ideal for the adventurous.

There are facilities to be found on the shores of the loch and there are hotels in the area. Climbing back into the hills once more, the road curves round above the head of Loch Maree, providing yet another memorable view, before gradually dropping down a tortuous route through the glen to Gairloch.

Ledgowan Lodge Hotel: Tel 01445720252

Gairloch

A LITTLE fishing village on the Atlantic coast of Ross-shire (Gair means short, thus a small loch), Gairloch has become a favoured resort among discriminating holiday-makers wishing to get away from it all.

Once almost unknown outside the Highlands, Gairloch was used during World War II as a gathering place for convoys. Now it is a resort with a golf course, a long sandy beach, several hotels and chalet parks. At Gairloch Chandlery and the Marine Life Centre, cruises can be taken to watch whales, porpoises and dolphins. There is a Leisure Centre that includes a climbing wall, fitness room and tennis courts. The Solas Art Gallery is open through the summer, as is Gairloch Heritage Museum. The harbour is still in use though now mainly by yacht traffic.

In the short summer nights, entertainment can be found in the hotels and at public venues in the vicinity.

Heritage Museum: Tel 01445 712287
Gairloch Chandlery: Tel 01445 712458
Gairloch Marine Life: Tel 01445 712636
Gairloch Golf Club: Tel 01445 712407
Leisure Centre: Tel 01445 712345
Solas Gallery: Tel 01445 712626

Inverewe Gardens

TRAVELLING over the headland beyond Gairloch, the road drops down to Loch Ewe and the village of Poolewe. Here at the Poolewe Hotel, Mrs MacKenzie, wife of Osgood MacKenzie watched the progress of the construction of one of the most famous gardens in Britain at Inverewe.

Legend has it that Osgood, having married her, assumed control of her fortune and started developing his obsession, the Garden at Inverewe. She gave birth to a daughter within a year. As soon as she could be separated from her mother, the baby was put into the charge of a nurse and her mother was banished from Inverewe. She stayed at Poolewe House across the loch for the rest of her life, only seeing her daughter as she grew up from a distance, a vague figure glimpsed in the developing garden.

The gardens are a tribute to the single-minded dedication of Osgood MacKenzie and his daughter, who later passed the gardens over to the National Trust for Scotland. The Trust still maintain and develop the garden.

National Trust for Scotland Inverewe Gardens:Tel 01445 781229
Poolewe Hotel: Tel 01445 781241

Altbea

FROM here the road passes over another peninsula to the other part of the loch. Once more there are spectacular views, this time over the sea beyond the Isle of Ewe with the distant Summer Isles scattered on the horizon. The idea of the Summer Isles does raise images of sun drenched beaches and lazy days sipping cold drinks in the soft summer air. The truth is that the islands got their name from their use by farmers for summer grazing of cattle and sheep.

There is a perfume studio, (run by the only Perfumers in Scotland) complete with café and a distillery, the Loch Ewe Distillery known as the only legal illicit still in Scotland.

The road runs along the face of the cliff, past the naval refuelling base to the village of Altbea. Here the road crosses yet another point to Gruinard Bay. There is a viewpoint, as the bay comes into view, at the top of a steep drop down to sea level.

The bay contains the infamous Gruinard Island used during World War II to test the effects of anthrax. The island has since been de-contaminated and though sheep graze the island, guided tours have not been initiated as yet.

Loch Ewe Distillery: Tel 01445 731242
Perfume Studio and Aroma Café: Tel 01445 731618

Strath Mor

Leaving the sandy beaches of Gruinard Bay, the road
turns inland for about five miles to the shores of Little
Loch Broom. It then follows the Loch inland for another
five miles, before climbing gradually up through the
Dundonnell Forest. A viewpoint on the left of the road
gives a glimpse of Strath Mor with Loch Broom visible.
The road then curves round to join the A886 at Corrieshalloch Gorge and Falls. Turning left there is a layby
with toilets on the right and a path to the left of the road
that goes down to the precarious bridge over the falls.
The last twelve miles to Ullapool are through increasingly
softer land, the strath levels out and houses become more
frequent. Situated in the curve of the headland that partly
encloses Loch Broom, the town of Ullapool is sheltered
from the direct winds of the Atlantic and is a safe haven
for boats.

Ullapool

ULLAPOOL was for many years famed as a fishing port. Created by the Fisheries Association in 1788, its purpose was to further the herring industry. Though for many years it prospered in fishing, sadly it does no longer. It enjoyed a brief renaissance during the 1990s when factory ships from Eastern Europe and the Soviet Union based themselves in the area. However, because of its location in a superb mountain region, it also enjoyed a reputation among walkers and climbers and has always been a base for exploring. It is also the port of the main ferry link to Stornoway on the Isle of Lewis.

There is a local museum and visitor centre and a golf course that welcomes visitors. The selection of shops ranges from supermarket to clothing, craft and bookshops. The

Ullapool Bookshop has an excellent selection of books and provides internet access for visitors.

The town is well supplied with hotels and guest accommodation. Visitors come to enjoy climbing the many spectacular mountains. Offshore the Summer Isles are visible and in summer, trips are available to visit the islands by motor boat. The sheltered waters are a haven for visiting yachts and whilst this is not a beach resort and the weather can be uncertain, to stand on the hillside above Ullapool on a clear summer day is an experience never to be forgotten.

Calmac Ferries: Tel 01854 612258
Ullapool Museum: Tel 01845 612987
Summer Queen Cruises: Tel 01854 612472
Ullapool Golf Club: Tel 01854 613323
Ullapool Bookshop: Tel 01854 612918

The Way Back

THE ROUTE back to Inverness is the A886 past the Corrieshalloch Falls, climbing up across the moor to Loch Glasnacardoch, a reservoir created for the hydro electric system. The loch is situated in a glen at the lower end of which is a dam. Interestingly the Aultguish Inn is located almost under the dam wall on the left of the road. The road continues, dropping down into Strath Garve past Inchbae Lodge on the right sitting against the mountain slope. The Black Water river runs down beside the road and into Loch Garve. The road continues through Garve to Inverness.

Aultguish Inn: Tel 01997 455254

Otter

Thurso, Wick and John o'Groats

THE ROAD north from Inverness crosses the Kessock Bridge and the Black Isle. The road is good at this point and passes through green farmlands. There is a causeway across the Cromarty Firth and the road follows the shore for fifteen miles before turning inland for the stretch through to Tain and the Dornoch Firth. The causeway across the Firth has been open for several years and has shortened the journey north considerably. The scenery is quite pleasant rolling country with glimpses of the sea becoming more frequent as you progress northward.

To the east are Dornoch and Embo with their sandy beaches, then Skibo Castle, though not signposted, lies tucked away in the woods. The road swings around the shores of Loch Fleet, with views out across the North Sea, before briefly leaving the shoreline only to rejoin it just short of Golspie. High on the hill to the left of the

Causeway, Dornoch

road can be seen the tall statue of the unpopular Duke of Sutherland. During the Highland clearances in the nineteenth century, the estate factors dealt harshly with the crofters and the Duke was blamed for their excesses.

The main road in the town of Golspie is mostly lined with shops and hotels paralleling the shore. Facilities include a golf course, bathing beach and fishing, all within easy reach. Parking is off the road on the left halfway through the town. The railway line to Wick runs through the town with an additional station just to the north at Dunrobin Castle, seat of the Duke of Sutherland.

Dunrobin Castle

Dunrobin Castle

THE LARGEST house north of Inverness is Dunrobin Castle. The earliest part of the structure is said to be thirteenth century. The latest restorations by Sir Robert Lorimer included designing the library, drawing rooms and the dining room. The castle was at one time used as a boys' boarding school before reverting to its current role as the home of the Duke and seat of the Clan Sutherland

Designed on the lines of a French chateau, it stands in extensive gardens inspired by those at Versailles, laid out in 1850 by architect Sir Charles Barry, who also designed the Houses of Parliament.

The Castle has been occupied continuously since it was built and contains many beautiful objects throughout its elegant interior. The stunning Gardens are host to regular falconry displays throughout the season.

Dunrobin Castle: Tel 01408 633177

Brora

FROM Golspie, continue along the coast to the town of Brora. Featuring a sandy beach, salmon and trout fishing, golf course plus the Clyneleish Distillery, this former coal mining and fishing community now depends on tourism. The beaches along the coast at this point provide ideal basking sites for seals and it is not unusual to see hundreds covering some of the less used beaches along the shore.

Brora Golf Club: Tel 01408 621417
Clynelish Distillery: Tel 01408 623000

Helmsdale

HELMSDALE is bigger than Brora and boasts a fine Telford Bridge across the river. There is the Timespan Heritage Centre complete with a riverside café on the left of the road and it is where the A897 goes off the A9 along the Strath of Kildonan, to Portskerra on the north coast. The road splits there, east to Thurso and John o'Groats, west to Tongue and Durness (for Cape Wrath).

At the mouth of the Strath now stands the bronze statue erected by Canadian businessman, Dennis MacLeod. It depicts a Highlander with his son commemorating those Highland folk who emigrated during the Highland Clearances.

Timespan: Tel 01432 821327

The A9 continues north following the coast through several spectacular twists and turns and climbs through small communities. Between Dunbeath and Latheron is the Laidhay Croft Museum (open during the summer) and the village of Latheron marks the junction for the direct route to Thurso, avoiding the longer journey via Wick.

Wick

THE LAST seventeen miles to Wick are mainly along the coastline. The road is fairly good and arriving at Wick, the industrial nature of the town is a contrast to the pastoral countryside beside the sea. The impression of bustle is heightened by the presence of the new supermarket on the outskirts. There is a fishing fleet in Wick harbour, though much depleted in these times. The Caithness Glass company originated here. The airport just north of town, and the proximity of John o'Groats, Gills Bay and Scrabster, makes onward travel to Orkney and Shetland quite easy.

John o'Groats

FROM Wick the A9 continues north to Duncansby Head and John o'Groats. The ferry at John o'Groats is passenger only; for cars it is necessary to use the Pentland ferry from Gills Bay or the Northlink Ferry from Scrabster.

The name John o'Groats came from the original ferry operator in the sixteenth century. John de Groot, a Dutchman started the ferry and ran it with his eight sons. Because of the strife between his sons, he built his house with eight sides, eight doors and an eight-sided dining table, this so that none could claim precedence over the other. There is a mound and flagpole where their house once stood. The Viking influence is still strong here and many of the placenames reflect this. Wick for instance, comes from *Vik* (bay). Thurso (bull's river *Norse*) also was recorded as *Thorsa* in the twelfth century and could also be Viking in origin. Scrabster (rocky farmstead) is almost certainly Viking.

The Pentland Firth that washes the northern shores of Scotland is a special stretch of water. Renowned for its powerful currents, the waters are a stunning bright blue in the sunshine but brooding and menacing under lowering cloud.

Castle of Mey

BETWEEN John o'Groats and Thurso is Gills Bay (4 miles) and shortly beyond is the turnoff for the Castle of Mey (possibly from the Norse, castle of seagulls). The home of the Earls of Caithness, the Sinclair family lived in the castle until the death of the last Earl in 1889. The family was known for its more eccentric members and it is recorded that in 1860 the fourteenth Earl brought the first steam car to the district at that time.

The castle declined from 1889 until 1952 when the late Queen Mother purchased it as her home. Her loving restoration makes it one of the sights of the north. Now owned by the Prince of Wales, he has continued the work undertaken by his grandmother. The grounds and castle are open to the public.

Castle of Mey: Tel 01847 851473

From here the road passes through the village of Dunnet. A mixture of Gaelic and Norse, the name means the fort on the headland. At this point it is possible to drive up to the most northerly point on the mainland of Britain at Dunnet Head. Dominating the surrounding area, the Stephenson lighthouse is a tribute to the quality of the engineering that built it.

A Visitor Centre dedicated to the flora and fauna of the area can be found at Dunnet village.

Dunnet Visitor Centre: Tel 01847 821531

Wild Poppy

Crossbill

Silver Birch

Thurso

Scrabster lighthouse

THURSO lies at the head of Thurso Bay and out on the western arm lies Scrabster, the ferry port, with the lighthouse beyond. From here the ferry to Stromness in the Orkney Islands runs on a regular timetable. To the east the land stretches out to Dunnet Head

The town of Thurso stands on the Thurso River. Salmon and trout are fished in its waters. A settlement has been at this location from the seventh century, the Norse influence being at its height in the eleventh century under the rule of Thorfinn. To the north can be seen the ruin of Thurso Castle, once home of the Ulbster branch of the Sinclair family. Harold's Tower marks the family burial ground believed to be built over the grave of Earl Harold, past ruler of half the Orkney and Shetland Isles and half of present-day Caithness. The town museum is a ready source of information on this and other historic facts.

The Swanson Art Gallery can be found at the Thurso Library and the Strathnaver Museum tells the story of the Highland Clearances at Strathnaver. The Dounreay Visitor Centre shows the history of the famous nuclear power station.

The many early Georgian houses in Thurso are reminiscent of the New Town of Edinburgh.

The population has fluctuated with the contraction of the fishing industry and the coming and going of the atomic energy plant at Dounreay. It is the end of the railway line and the most northerly town on mainland Britain. Surrounded by wild lonely moors, it's worth a visit, especially if en-route to the Orkney Isles.

Strathnaver Museum: Tel 01641 521418
Dounreay Visitor Centre: Tel 01847 806086
NorthLink Ferries: Tel 0845 6000 449

Because of the distances involved, the return journey is suggested using the direct road to Latheron. The A895 runs almost due south from Thurso for 23 miles through moorland and low hills. The rolling landscape is largely peatland covered with heather, though it is becoming punctuated by windmills in groups, generating electricity. This is not the most scenic journey and the road not the best, but it can be traversed in half an hour. From Latheron to Inverness is a reverse of the journey north.

The Black Isle

JUST NORTH of Inverness, on the other side of the Moray Firth, is the Black Isle. Not actually an island, the peninsula is renowned for its rich soil and soft rolling countryside. The name derived from its lack of snow in the winter, the former name was Ardmeanach (wooded ridge) which is still used for the wooded ridge that runs down the peninsula.

Mainly farm land with forest, the area has been cultivated for hundreds of years. Its proximity to Inverness has made it a favourite holiday region. Cross the Kessock Bridge and take the right turn to Munlochy on the B9161 to start a leisurely drive through the mixed woods and farmlands of the south side of the Black Isle.

Just past the village of Munlochy is the A832. Turn right past the head of Munlochy Bay for the village of Avoch (pronounced Och). Once a fishing village Avoch is now mainly used by pleasure craft. To the south-west on a mound is the ruin of Ormond Castle, which was once the home of Andrew de Moray, who together with William Wallace led the Scots to victory at Stirling Bridge.

At Rosehaugh just to the north-west was the seat of the 'Bluidy MacKenzie'. Sir George MacKenzie, former Lord Advocate, was renowned for his harsh treatment of the Covenanters in the late 1600s.

From Avoch the road runs along the through wooded

shore to Fortrose and Rosemarkie. At Fortrose, Chanonry Point with the lighthouse marks the division between the inner and outer waters of the Moray Firth. Just a mile away across the Firth is Fort George. A ferry once connected the two places.

The ruined cathedral was founded by David I for the See of Ross in the eleventh century with later additions. The clock tower bell dates from 1460. In 1880 a horde of silver coins dating from the reign of Robert III (1337-1406) was discovered buried in the cathedral green.

The small town of Rosemarkie has a fine beach and impressive cliffs and is a well-known holiday resort with a church dedicated to St Boniface and said to date from the eighth century. The small Groam House museum has a unique collection of Pictish history based around the famous Symbol stone that stood beside the church. From Rosemarkie the road shows the bright yellow fields of rape contrasting with the sombre green of the pinewoods.

Groam House Museum: Tel 01381 620961

Cromarty

THE TOWN of Cromarty is several centuries old but truly came into its own in the eighteenth century with the construction of the harbour and the establishment of the cloth and lace industries. As a port it gained importance as a major link with Scandinavian countries. Famous now for its courthouse, which is a museum complete with a court and memorabilia, and its association with Hugh Millar, the nineteenth century scientist, this charming town is full of old houses and narrow lanes. The Gallery Tea Room is a bookshop and art gallery where tea is served in a room with walls hung with local art and photography. Elsewhere, the harbour and waterfront provide room to walk and take in the views across the Firth to Nigg and out to sea through the channel.

The return trip along the Cromarty Firth is a calm easy drive through the green countryside, passing through small settlements with the waters of the Cromarty Firth gleaming on the right.

The sign 'Jemimaville' can be found just a few miles from Cromarty. The community was named for the lady who was settled there after her father had become fed-up with the quarrelling between Jemima and her sister Barbara. Jemima was settled on Cromarty and her sister was settled in Barbaraville on the northern shore of the Firth, separating the two sisters once and for all.

To extend this excursion, it could be possible to cross the Firth to Nigg and journey up the picturesque Tarbat peninsula to Balintore on the Moray Firth. Once a fishing village, the small harbour became popular with sea anglers. Now there is a further feature of interest – the bronze mermaid statue on the beach at Balintore is well worth seeing. There are fine cliff walks and views and the remains of the Chapel in Hilton of Cadboll is of historic interest. The road can be followed up to Tarbat Ness before returning through Tain to the A9 for the return to Inverness via the Cromarty Causeway.

Cromarty Courthouse: Tel 01381 600418

The Royal South

Daviot Church

THE MAIN road south is the A9. Initially it is a fine dual carriageway and passes the picturesque church at Daviot, where the ashes of Alastair MacLean were scattered after the author's premature death in 1987. To the right is the turnoff to the old military road to Fort Augustus which follows Strath Nairn south westward.

A few miles further, the road having reverted to one-lane, the Tomatin distillery can be seen, and visited, on the right. The largest single malt whisky producer in the country, Tomatin provides an important contribution to blended whiskies throughout Scotland.

The visitor centre at Tomatin makes no charge for the distillery tour and as is usual, a small taste of the product is provided.

From Tomatin, the road winds on through the forested countryside and rises towards the Grampian mountains, continuing southward to Pitlochry, Perth and the Central Lowlands.

Tomatin Distillery: Tel 01808 511444

Lairg and Beyond

FROM INVERNESS the road to Lairg is once more the A9. North, across the Kessock Bridge, past the Black Isle and the Cromarty Firth, follow the shore to the turnoff to Alness. This road winds its way over Struie Hill, at first through green fields, then through rougher country until it becomes high moorland backed by pine plantations with views over the Dornoch Firth. Once over the shoulder of Struie Hill there are views over the Kyle of Sutherland.

At the road junction, turn left to Bonar Bridge. This is a coat hanger bridge across the River Oykel at the Vale of Sutherland. Turn left here still following the A836. This road follows the river to Carbisdale Castle seen over the river on the hill opposite.

Carbisdale Castle

Carbisdale Castle

CARBISDALE Castle was built in the early part of the twentieth century for the Duchess of Sutherland. The Duke had married her against the wishes of his family and having left her everything in his will, the family contested the legality. However an agreement was reached which included a suitable dwelling to be situated outside Sutherland. She elected to have her house built on the rise of land above the waters of the Kyle of Sutherland, over the county boundary, but overlooking her former home. It was sold to the Salvesen family in the thirties and it was home to the Norwegian Royal Family during World War II. After the war the Salvesen heir gave it to the Scottish Youth Hostels Association. This beautiful building is one of the grandest hostels in Britain.

Carbisdale marks the scene of the last battle fought by the Marquis of Montrose during the campaign against the Covenanters in 1650. Montrose's army comprised 2000 men from Orkney. Though they were big strapping Vikings, they unfortunately had never encountered horses used in battle. The Covenanter cavalry proved too much for the inexperienced Orkneymen who broke and ran. This defeat and subsequent capture of Montrose at Ardvreck Castle marked the end of the campaign for the Royalist Army in Scotland.

Carbisdale Castle: Tel 0870 155 3255

Ben Loyal

Here there are two choices – the main road, or by following the river another mile, the Shin Falls road. The latter allows a visit to the salmon leap at Shin. There is a visitor centre at Shin Falls operated by the Harrods owner and local landowner, Mohammed al Fayed. Further on, the A836 briefly follows the shore of Loch Shin before continuing north to Tongue. For the next 38 miles there is only moorland and hills. Eventually there is Altnaharra, a village and hotel at the foot of Loch Naver with Ben Kubreck towering on the right of the road.

From here the country becomes more and more interesting with small lochs and bigger hills and even the odd house. Ahead, the heights of Ben Loyal loom up to meet the clouds while the waters of Loch Loyal rim the right side of the road. It is possible here to see the ocasional fisherman wielding his salmon rod thigh-deep in the chilly waters. The Loch Loyal lodge can be seen halfway up the Loch on the left. Shortly after the head of the loch, the waters of the Kyle of Tongue appear bisected by the causeway that connects the two banks.

The Causeway at Tongue

Tongue

THE VILLAGE of Tongue lies on the shore of the Kyle of Tongue. On the promontory west of the village stands the ruin of Castle Varrick, believed to be the home of an eleventh century Norse king. Tongue House, on the Thurso road, was once the seat of the Mackays though the house passed to the Duke of Sutherland in the early eighteenth century.

Here the road joins the A838 which crosses the causeway. It is worth a short diversion to Melness following the banks of the Kyle seawards past golden sands to the coast. The views are worth the effort and it is possible to send postcards from the remote Post Office overlooking yet another golden beach. The main road crosses the peninsula A' Mhoine to the villages of Hope and Eriboll on Loch Eriboll. The road passes round the Sea Loch on the way to Durness, on the north coast, the most northerly village on mainland Britain.

Durness

A SMALL place, though not without interest, the beach at Durness is a wide sweep of golden sand uncluttered by the usual debris of the shore. Swept by the waters of the north Atlantic, it is a favourite spot for visitors and locals.

There is an information office and a craft shop. There are two hotels and many local B&Bs and a small super-market to provide food, papers and Post Office services.

The Limestone cave 'Smoo Cave', once visited by Sir Walter Scott in 1814, is an awe-inspiring sight and there is a craft village at Balnakeil with different crafts in production.

The ruined church at Balnakeil has fine carved monuments of eighteenth and nineteenth century origin, and the older gravestones of Donald MacMhurchadh 1619 and the Gaelic poet Rob Donn 1714-1778. The raised area in the graveyard is the massed grave of the emigrants lost in the wreck of the *Canton* in 1849. Marked by a festival of music in his name, one of the enthusiastic

Balnakeil Church

visitors to Durness was John Lennon. Following visits as a boy, he never lost his affection for this small village on the edge of the land.

Cape Wrath lighthouse

Cape Wrath

AT THE EXTREME north-west point of the mainland of Britain, the Cape is located at a spot where south-westerly currents meet the flow from the north and winds combine to create a turmoil of conflicting elements. The name Cape Wrath seems apt for such a wild and stormy spot, however the name has a much more prosaic meaning. It comes from the Old Norse and translates as the 'turning point', being the Cape where the marauding Norsemen turned southward to raid the west coast of Scotland. The lighthouse on the point can be seen for twenty seven miles and from the headland the reefs below can be seen. The reefs are the haunt of a mass of seabirds (mainly Gannets) usually present at this last place in Scotland.

The lighthouse is a Stephenson Light, one of the many lights on the west coast of Scotland built by the famous family of Robert Louis Stephenson. Standing below the trumpet of the now defunct fog horn, it is possible to look straight down the cliff below.

From Durness (the headland of the deer) it is possible during the summer to visit Cape Wrath via a ferry and by minibus. Having said that, the ferry is a small motorboat that crosses the Kyle of Durness in just a few minutes, providing the water is not too rough, and the tide high enough to allow the boat to come alongside the quay. On the other side of the Kyle the bus awaits: a twelve seat

coach which departs up what seems to be an impossibly steep slope over a road that was last surfaced over fifty years ago. There is a forty minute journey to the lighthouse on the point. The road does not improve, the driver's interesting and humorous commentary on the history of the locality sometimes interrupted by an eagle launching itself from the cliff below, or perhaps the appearance of some of the other wildlife. There is a herd of red deer roaming the Cape and it is suspected the coach driver has an arrangement with them to appear conveniently at some time during the coach journey.

Of the three houses that can be seen, two are holiday

homes, the other is derelict. No one lives on the Cape now, though at one time over thirty people, in addition to the lighthouse crew and their families, lived and crofted there. There was even a one-room school, the ruins of which can be seen beside the first MoD barrier for the firing range. The firing range at Cape Wrath is the only surviving range of this type still in use. It is used by both UK and European forces. Whilst there are no munitions fired at the Cape itself, aircraft fly over targeting the small island offshore.

Wren

Cape Wrath Ferry Services: Tel 01971 511376
Cape Wrath Mini bus: Tel 01971 511343

The Way South

FROM DURNESS, the way south is on the A838 to Rhiconich where a side trip to Kinlochbervie is possible. Sadly this fishing port which experienced a renaissance during the 1980-1990s, with large harbour developments for fish handling and distribution, has regressed owing to the dramatic cuts in permitted catches. The facilities are now grossly underused by as few as three boats per week, where once dozens called to offload their catch.

The road continues onward past Laxford Bridge where the A838 goes off to the left to follow Loch Stack, Loch Mor and Loch Shin, to Lairg and back to Inverness.

The A894 carries on down the coast to Scourie, once just a crofting village with angling facilities, now better known for the bird sanctuary on the Island of Handa. The journey south continues, generally following the coast through hilly and mountainous countryside. The mighty Quinaig dominates the skyline ahead. Just beyond Kylestrome, the elegant Kylesku bridge crosses Loch Glendhu on the way to the junction with the A869 where a diversion to Lochinver by the coastal route can be taken.

This is a switchback road with extensive views of the islands and offshore rocks, passing the headland out to the Point of Stoer where the sea stack, the Old Man of Stoer can be found.

The community at Lochinver gives the impression of

a busy holiday oriented spot. There is the Cabarfeidh Restaurant with its famous pie shop renowned for the widest variety of pie fillings, it's believed, in Scotland. (Boar and Apricot?)

There is also a most helpful Tourist Bureau located on the sea front.

The direct route back to the main road south runs along the shores of Loch Assynt, a picturesque loch with Quinag on the left and Ben Garbh across the loch on the right.

Cabarfeidh Restaurant: Tel 01571 844321
Tourist Information: Tel 0845 225 5121

Ardvreck Castle

AT THE FAR end of Loch Assynt stands the ruined Ardvreck Castle. On a peninsula, almost an island, this historic castle makes a most romantic picture. Dating from the fifteenth century, it was the seat of the MacLeods of

Assynt. It was here in 1650 that the Marquis of Montrose was taken as a captive, after the Battle of Carbisdale, before being carried to Edinburgh to be executed. The castle was more or less abandoned after a major siege in 1672.

A little way along the mainland shore from the castle is the ruin of Calda House built in the 1720s by the MacKenzie owners of Assynt. The expense of the building was responsible in part for the bankruptcy of MacKenzie and the house was destroyed within ten years of its construction.

The village of Inchnadamph has a hotel and stands in one of the most geologically interesting areas in the world. The Archaean Gneiss rock is one of the oldest and is only found elsewhere in the Outer Hebrides and north of the St Lawrence River in Canada.

Travelling south the distinctive mountains of Suilven, Cul Mor and Stac Polly march along the skyline to the west. Another junction with the A835 at Ledmore allows a direct route down Strath Oykel to link with the A836 just north of Lairg. The road to Ullapool continues as the A835.

Stac Polly

The return route to Inverness is directly down the A835, past the Glasnacardoch Reservoir over the moorland mentioned in the section on Ullapool. Beyond the Aultguish Hotel the country begins to soften, highlighting the difference between the velvety green cultivated fields and the wild moorland area where past cultivation has reverted to its natural state. The comparison is quite dramatic. The gentle tailored beauty of the hedged, fenced or walled fields gives way to coarse grass, heather, and reed gorse and broom of the moor. Each has its own beauty, but each has its own ecology, and as more crofts go untended, the face of the land changes.

From Garve, the road passes Blackwater Loch and gradually descends past Rogie Falls, the softer country around Contin unrolls and the green fields either side of the River Conon herald the return to Inverness.

Aultguish Hotel: Tel 01997 455254

seascape

The Land

THE FACE of the landscape changes north of Inverness, rolling flatlands in the east, the central area largely moorland and forest, and to the west the mountains extending northwards to Cape Wrath. The spectacular west coast scenery is favoured by walkers and climbers. The road system is based on the contours of the country, winding through glens, over passes and saddles and clinging to the edges of cliffs. It can be exciting motoring. In addition, the spectacular landscape of sea, mountains and shore; empty golden sandy beaches washed by the blue waters of the Atlantic – sounds as idyllic as it sometimes really can be. However it can also be exhilaratingly rough, with gale force winds snatching your breath.

The central area is not nearly as spectacular. But to those who know the country, its appeal is in the long lonely roads through the empty moor and marsh lands. The narrow roads lend the feeling of remoteness despite being at most only nineteen miles from civilization.

The east coast, though in parts spectacular and often beautiful, is much more settled. With towns and villages scattered all along the North Sea coast, the landscape of castles, farms and historic sites, lies along well maintained roads and is served by rail links. A much more tailored landscape than the centre and west, but nonetheless interesting and worth visiting.

The People

THE MOST famously known early people of the north are the Picts. Museums in the Black Isle and the Moray coast all have information of these early inhabitants; but succeeding peoples have left a far greater footprint on the land. Both east and west coasts suffered regular visits from the fierce Norsemen in their dreaded longships.

Many fierce and bloody skirmishes were fought along both coastlines from the fifth century. The raiders were followed by armies who took possession of land which they then settled, to become part of the Scotland of today. Thus the people became mixed with the Vikings from the north. From the south and west, the influx of Saxon (Sassenach) and Scots from Hibernia (Ireland) created a vigorous population.

The language spoken because of the turmoil created by the shifting populations became a melange of different sources and accents. The once widely spoken Pictish tongue of the Highland peoples was overtaken by first, the Gaelic speech of the invading Scots, and subsequently the lingua franca of the Saxon, Angle and French.

Pictish is no longer spoken and in fact has disappeared from even scholarly sources. The renewed interest in the study of Gaelic has ensured its survival, though its usage is still confined to a small proportion of the population.

The Waters

THE MOST dramatic waters of this region are probably those of the Pentland Firth. Ranging from deep slate grey on a dour day to brilliant cobalt blue in the sunshine, the fast flowing waters of the Firth have been the main sea route between the North Sea and the Atlantic Ocean. From Duncansby to Dunnet the currents in these waters have tested the finest sailors and bested many. The Orkney Islands to the north channel the water, causing unique conditions. From the lighthouse at Duncansby Head to the east through to Dunnet Head at the western end, this stretch of water has always constituted a challenge to sailors of all nations.

The North Sea coast to the east contains large areas of comparatively shallow water. Such variations in depth can always be tricky as they create constantly changing conditions. The shoreline of sandy beaches and rugged cliffs are a testament to the power of wind and wave and their effect on the land. There are a series of harbours along the east coast available to give shelter to cruising yachts, if needed

The Atlantic coast to the west is dramatic with cliffs, stacks and incredibly long deserted sandy beaches. The coast is also influenced by the waters of the Gulf Stream. The rugged shoreline is distinguished by many secluded bays and sea lochs sheltering small fishing ports, once prosperous though now surviving mainly on tourism. Popular with yachtsmen who enjoy the sailing through the Hebrides and along the coast, the Atlantic shores provide breathtaking scenery. Inland there is a selection of lochs and rivers, popular with fishermen and sailors alike.

Strathspey railway

The Railways

FOR MANY centuries, sea lochs and long coast-lines allowed transport by water, but the arrival of the age of steam heralded a new era in communication in Scotland. This was particularly true in the Highlands where roads were poor and in places non-existent.

All the routes north of the Glasgow-Edinburgh line, are single-track; passing is normally at stations. Because of the spectacular scenery through which the tracks were laid, rail enthusiasts have been encouraged to travel the routes. The Jacobite, possibly better known for its links with the Harry Potter films on the Fort William-Mallaig line, is a good example of the reintroduction of steam.

In the case of the Strathspey railway, the line between Aviemore and Broomhill has been reinstated by enthusiasts, with plans to extend to Grantown on Spey in the future. Broomhill station is the location of 'Glenbogle' station used in the TV series 'Monarch of the Glen'. The station still carries the Glenbogle signboard. The narrow gauge Mull railway runs from Craignure to Torosay Castle in the summer. Special steam excursions are run throughout the Scotrail system from time to time and companies like Railtrail Tours and the Royal Scotsman specialise in this form of rail travel.

The port termini link with the inter-island ferries, once part of an integrated rail-bus-ferry system that was the norm through the pre-World War II period. Now on the west coast Highland line, only Oban and Mallaig have ferry links, though Kyle of Lochalsh which is now joined to the Isle of Skye by the Skye Bridge was once served by ferry. To the north, Thurso, Gills Bay and John o'Groats all provide ferry services to Orkney, though the rail link goes only as far as Thurso.

Strathspey Steam Railway: Tel 01479 810725
The Jacobite (Fort William-Mallaig): Tel 01542 737751/53
Railtrail Tours Ltd: Tel 01538 382323
The Royal Scotsman: Tel 0845 077 2222
Scotrail: Tel 0845 601 5929